LET'S DRAW STEP BY STEP

Let's Draw
JUNGLE
ANIMALS

KASIA DUDZIUK

WINDMILL
BOOKS

Published in 2020 by Windmill Books,
an Imprint of Rosen Publishing
29 East 21st Street, New York, NY 10010

Copyright © Arcturus Holdings Ltd, 2020

Cataloging-in-Publication Data

Names: Dudziuk, Kasia.
Title: Let's draw jungle animals / Kasia Dudziuk.
Description: New York : Windmill Books, 2020. | Series: Let's draw step by step | Includes glossary and index.
Identifiers: ISBN 9781538391365 (pbk.) | ISBN 9781538391389 (library bound) | ISBN 9781538391372 (6 pack)
Subjects: LCSH: Jungle animals in art--Juvenile literature. | Drawing--Technique--Juvenile literature.
Classification: LCC NC783.8.J85 D839 2019 | DDC 743.6--dc23

Manufactured in the United States of America

CPSIA Compliance Information: Batch BS19WM: For Further Information contact Rosen Publishing, New York, New York at 1-800-237-9932

Contents

Let's Draw!

Welcome to the world of drawing! In this book you'll learn how to draw all sorts of jungle animals in four easy steps. All you need is a pencil and paper, and some crayons, colored pencils, or markers for coloring in.

Tiger

1 Start with the head and ears.

2 Now add a body and legs.

3 Don't forget to draw the long tail and tummy!

4 Add a face, orange fur, and some cool, black stripes.

Monkey

1 Your monkey has a round head and big ears.

2 Add the body and front legs.

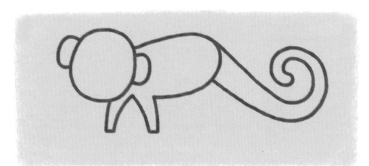

3 Now draw a long, curly tail, so it can swing through the trees!

4 Draw the back legs, face, and paws. Color it in shades of brown.

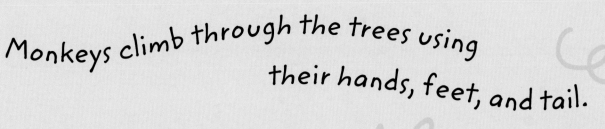

Monkeys climb through the trees using their hands, feet, and tail.

Chameleon

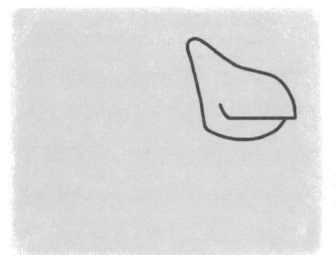

1 Begin with this wiggly shape for the head.

2 The top of the body is curved, but the bottom is straight.

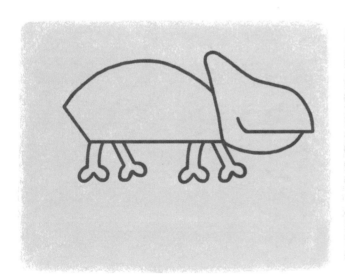

3 Draw four little legs.

4 Add a long tail and a big, round eye. Give it orange and green stripes.

Chameleons can use camouflage to hide just about anywhere!

This chameleon is blue and yellow.

This one is lime green and red.

Why not try a pink and purple striped one?

This chameleon is green and orange.

Tree Frog

1 Start with the head and big, round eyes.

2 Now it needs front legs and a body.

3 It has big, strong back legs for jumping!

4 Add the eyes and mouth, and color it in bright green.

Gorilla

1 First, draw the head and little ears.

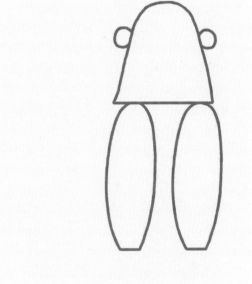

2 Add big front legs. They are very strong!

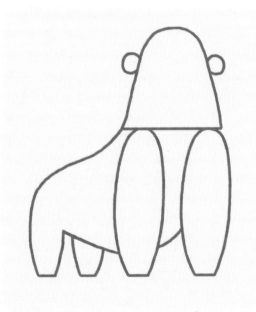

3 Draw this shape for the body and back legs.

4 Add a smiley face, pink paws, and black fur.

Anteater

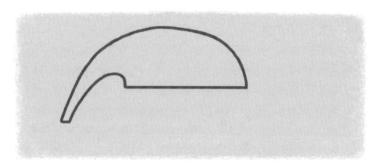

1 Here's the body and long snout.

2 Now add four little legs.

3 Add a long, thick tail.

4 Draw an eye, ears, feet, and a long, curly tongue. It's perfect for licking up all those ants!

Anteaters eat about 30,000 ants a day!

Jaguar

1 Begin by drawing the round head and ears.

2 Add front legs and paws.

3 Now draw the body and add a back leg.

4 Draw a curly tail, a happy face, and some little black spots.

Jaguars hunt at night. They watch their prey quietly, then they run and pounce!

This jaguar is sitting down.

This one is running very fast.

A jaguar with black fur is sometimes called a panther.

Cockatoo

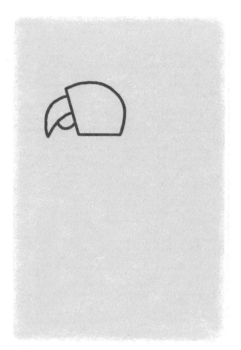

1 First, draw the head and beak.

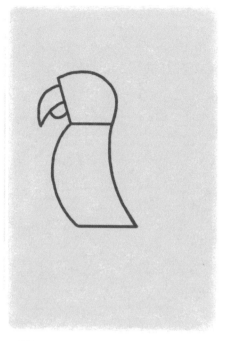

2 Add this shape for the body.

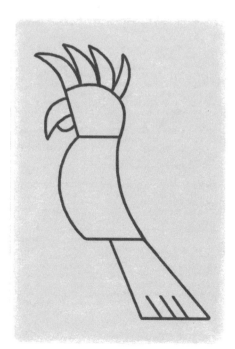

3 Don't forget the magnificent crest and tail feathers!

4 Draw an eye and a wing, then add orange feet and an orange beak. Color in white feathers and a yellow crest.

Hornbill

1 Start with this shape for the body.

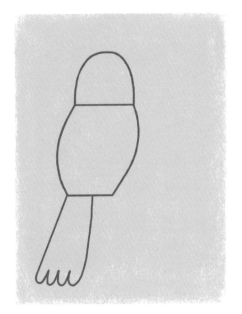

2 Add a head and a long, feathery tail.

3 Now draw the big bill. It's a very strange shape!

4 Draw an eye and little white feet. Finish the head and bill in bright shades.

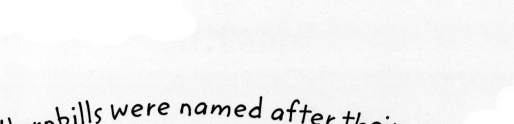

Hornbills were named after their big, hornlike bills.

Toucan

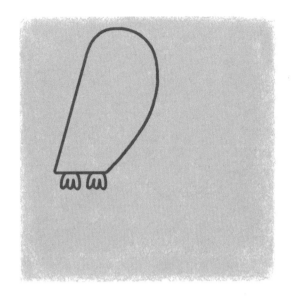

1 Draw this shape for the body, and add little feet.

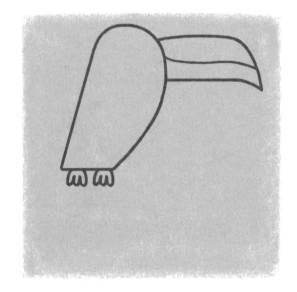

2 Draw a very big beak!

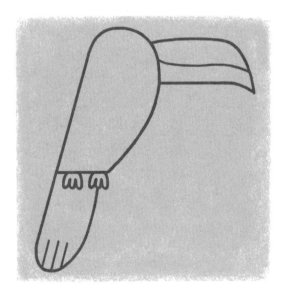

3 Add long tail feathers.

4 Draw a beady eye. Make the feathers black and white, and the beak red and orange.

Macaw

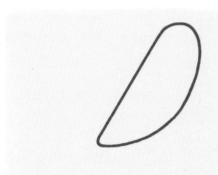

1 Start by drawing this shape for the body.

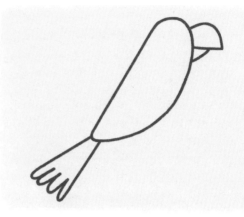

2 Now add a beak and tail feathers.

3 Draw the wings stretched out in flight.

4 Add eyes and feet. The feathers are bright red.

Lovebird

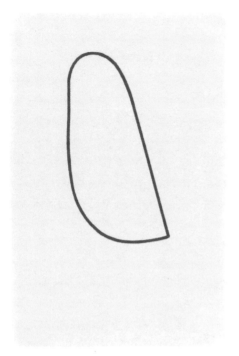

1 Start with this shape for the body.

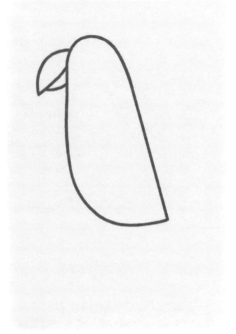

2 Now add the beak.

3 Draw a line across the chest, and add a tail.

4 Add an eye and little feet. Color it in bright shades of green and orange.

Lovebirds are a type of parrot.

When they find a mate, they spend all their time together.

Hummingbird

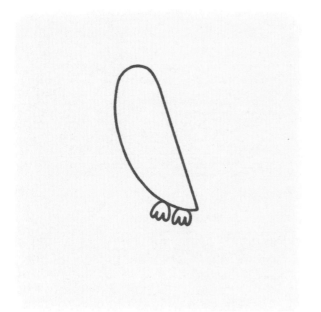

1 Begin with this shape for the body. Add tiny feet.

2 Draw the wings next. They are pointing backward.

3 Add a long, thin beak and a feathery tail.

4 Add a little eye. Finish the drawing in bright shades of blue, red, and green.

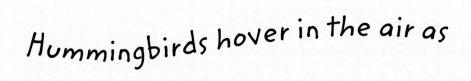

Hummingbirds hover in the air as they drink nectar from flowers.

Their wings beat so fast they make a humming sound.

Butterfly

1 First, draw a circle for the head.

2 Now add a long, thin body.

3 It needs four curved shapes for the lovely wings!

4 Add a happy face and some feelers. Make patterns on the wings and color it in pretty shades.

A butterfly starts life as a tiny egg. ⟶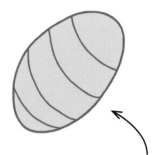

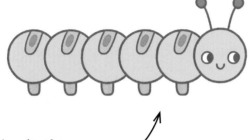

A wiggly
caterpillar comes
out of the egg.

The caterpillar
then changes into
a little case.

Later, a pretty
butterfly comes
out of the case.

Butterflies come in lots of different colors.

Spider

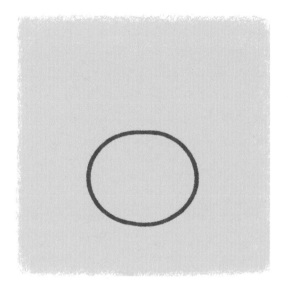

1 First, draw a round shape for the head.

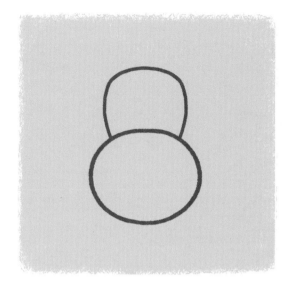

2 Now draw the body.

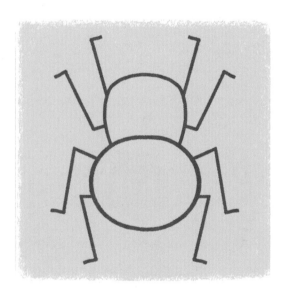

3 It has eight thin legs!

4 Add the face and make the body black. The spider's not all that scary, is it?

Spiders build webs using silk made in their bellies.

Add some fangs and hair and you will have a tarantula.

Glossary

beak A part of the mouth that sticks out on some animals and is used to tear food.

bill Another word for a bird's beak.

camouflage Patterns or colors that help an animal to hide by blending in with its surroundings.

crest A showy tuft or growth on the top of some animals' heads.

fangs Pointed teeth.

feelers The tentacles, or parts of a creature that help it to sense things around it.

fur The hairy coat of a mammal.

mate The breeding partner of an animal.

nectar A sweet liquid made by plants.

paws The feet of an animal.

pounce To jump on something very quickly.

prey Animals that are eaten by other animals.

tail feathers The feathers at the end of a bird.

tarantula A family of large, hairy spiders.

webs Networks of silky threads.

Further Information

Books

Chambers, Ailin. *Animals*. New York, NY: Gareth Stevens, 2015.

Colich, Abby. *Drawing Wild Animals.* North Mankato, MN: Capstone Press, 2015.

Cuddy, Robbin. *Learn to Draw Rainforest & Jungle Animals*. Lake Forest, CA: Walter Foster Jr., 2012.

Walter Forest Jr. Creative Team. *All About Drawing Wild Animals & Exotic Creatures*. Lake Forest, CA: Walter Foster Jr., 2018.

Websites

www.artforkidshub.com/how-to-draw/animals
This website uses videos to show you how to draw everything from monkeys to hummingbirds.

www.easypeasyandfun.com/how-to-draw
Learn how to draw a spider, a frog, and an owl using video tutorials and printed templates.

Publisher's note to educators and parents: Our editors have carefully reviewed these websites to ensure that they are suitable for students. Many websites change frequently, however, and we cannot guarantee that a site's future contents will continue to meet our high standards of quality and educational value. Be advised that students should be closely supervised whenever they access the Internet.

Index